UP LATE

NICK LAIRD

Up Late

Poems

W. W. NORTON & COMPANY

Celebrating a Century of Independent Publishing

For information about permission to reproduce selections from this book, write to
Permissions, W. W. Norton & Company, Inc., 500 Fifth Avenue, New York, NY 10110

For information about special discounts for bulk purchases, please contact
W. W. Norton Special Sales at specialsales@wwnorton.com or 800-233-4830

Manufacturing by Lakeside Book Company

ISBN 978-1-324-06544-9

W. W. Norton & Company, Inc., 500 Fifth Avenue, New York, N.Y. 10110
www.wwnorton.com

W. W. Norton & Company Ltd., 15 Carlisle Street, London W1D 3BS

1 2 3 4 5 6 7 8 9 0

Contents

iii

Acknowledgements

Many thanks to the editors of *Poetry Ireland*, *Poetry Review*, *Granta*, *New York Review of Books*, *New Yorker*, *London Review of Books* and *Stinging Fly*, where many of these poems appeared previously.

'American Poem' was written for an Extinction Rebellion reading and protest, 'The Vocation' as a commission for Poetry Jukebox and the Belfast Literature Festival, and 'Modest Proposal' as a commission for BBC Radio 4 to commemorate Jonathan Swift's *A Modest Proposal*.

Many thanks to Norton – especially to Jill Bialosky and Drew Weitman – and to Don Paterson and Terrance Hayes for having a read of the manuscript. All love and thanks as always to Z.

UP LATE

i

Grief

In the jungle or dense forest
what can distance mean?
Space, to the dweller there,
is a successive net of places,
cages ringed by living palings,
lacking an overall structure,
and the same is true of time:
there are no seasons, no sky,
nothing beyond day and night.
Time like space is shallow:
neither past nor future hold
substantial interest, but continue
following the stream and you
presumably will come to sea.

Theodicy

A human is not such a perfect machine.
I didn't design it for interaction particularly
with other machines – not closely – not non-stop.
I made the campfire, for example, to be nature's
television but with a human being basically
I was thinking of a tree, of what a tree needs.
A root system, distance, light and air. Even living
you are tearing through something made not
of particles but of the relations between them.
This morning, it really does seem necessary
to tell you, I made the mist, lying above the contours
of the forest, take the precise shape of the remains
of a poster that boy is ripping from a plywood siding
on Rue du Regard in the sixth arrondissement.
As to the question of pain – why it hurts, why
sometimes we crave it – I have here a number
of promising leads but the matter is dark so-
called because it does not interact with light.
As you're aware there's no decent performance
without restraint. And all these polyphonic
symphonies it should not be possible to generate
by one person alone and yet – and yet – and yet
when any of you comes into my presence
the room takes on a new tone. I did my best
in the sense I didn't underestimate the depths
of tenderness an animal – almost any animal –
might stir in us like colour into paint. I gave you
that, and if I slept in a stone or slept in a bomb,
or slept over a brothel during the gold rush,
if I slept in a cave in the mountain of Ulrith –

what I dreamt of was myself as a child of three
or four stood on the top step, dressed for bed,
weeping inconsolably and still getting yelled at.

On a Paper Clip

To bend inward forever
shying from the world

and retrace the first curve
but at a greater distance,

letting the correct inflection
delineate an absence

with just sufficient tension
to hold the poems together.

Ultion

You know it is a sin to lift a rock from where it sits in the sun,
warming itself, and iniquity to leave the silver pen
uncapped or the big light lit,

that the punishment for chopping down an apple tree was death
when the holy fire came from rubbing apple sticks together,
and you gave up trying to sleep,

and by dawn were running down the Grand Union towpath
past dog shit and litter, an emptied handbag on a bench,
the dead swan floating in the plastic,

and beneath your feet the earth – that hostage, that exhausted
host – felt like it was accelerating in its spinning faster
and faster as it tried to shake us off.

Property

What I think I know about the sunset is
the trees appear to be rising in front of it,
rising in front of the brilliant, splintered,
overripe light towards animate clouds arrayed
and edged in greys and dusky pinks – a few blues,
damson, pastel – and that scalloping excellent white.
I didn't mention the green, the green that is
pushing itself everywhere, my being, and I was yes
slightly stoned, down in the gazebo, having sat
by the dam on the Mombaccus Creek smoking
for half an hour, waiting for the beaver to come back.
It did not. The only sound was a cardinal
in the trees and when overhead fourteen geese
honked me and headed south and now my children
up in Jackie's garden, arguing, ignoring the pleas
of the babysitter I am paying twenty dollars an hour.
I saw a red cardinal up at the car once one weekend
here last spring, so fiercely territorial his own
reflection in the wing mirror meant he spent
a good hour trying to repel the imaginary intruder.
I find sometimes I want all of it. The moment of
sunset. The beavers' architected dam. The colours.
The babysitter. The soundtrack of an endless
quarrel. An evening to go on and on burning.
Cocteau was asked if his home was on fire, what
one thing would he save? The fire, he said, only
the fire.

Sheep's Head

Earlier I opened the door on the light and the light
rain falling on the water, on the Volvo, on Vera's field
where the trio of cattle were waiting out the weather,

and the light was the light of nowhere, lacking source,
though it appeared to radiate upwards to be absorbed
by the sky, a slab of ruined pewter hanging over

the crib of the harbour where a mobile of gannets
angle, buffeted, tacking bright sails to the gusts of light
rain blowing in off the stroppy, slapping Atlantic.

Each gannet perfects gannetness by practising control
before collapse, the absolute drop, choreographing
a series of vanishings to stipple the dark roil.

As I check the post a spider abseils off the empty letterbox
pursued on his line by a few raindrops suant as
the chain of buoys set out for the mussel lines

that crest and dip but fail to advance on the fish farm
they point at, the new cage nets that took John Murphy
nigh on three years to reset after the last big storm.

The light rain darkens the Goat's Path and the deep lane
down to the Cove, the bite in the cliff, the ribbed jetty
and immense ring of the mooring, trapped and rusting

forever into nothing, flake by flake, and rain pocks
the brass plaque embedded in the rock where Farrell,
spinning for mackerel, got taken by a wave and drowned.

I hear the night the cage nets for the salmon got wrecked
the rain chucked itself in buckets at the panes
and the wind was stricken and wild in the chimney

and out there was an exit where only net was before,
and from the rip in the continuum fish thrashed out
into the churn and glitter spilt in liveried propulsion,

thousands separately nosing downwards to
dimensions of no end, out of the turmoil into a silent
malevolence where each creature preyed upon the other,

and nothing was safe, I guess, since it was October
and I'd stopped the sitting tinkering with phrases
for lunch, and was taking the library stairs two at a time

to get out into the city and cross the square to catch
the guy who plays Haydn on the grand piano
he and his bald friend wheel out from somewhere

into the sun every morning, and sitting on a bench
listening to him I felt then like I often felt – reprieved,
heading every direction, ready to eat something.

American Poem

I also hoped to visit tropical resorts
to feel the texture of expensive sadness.
I wanted to avoid slaughter by growing

so large I would not fit in the machine,
but thinking everything was magic
was the same as thinking nothing was:

magnets, racecraft, three card monte.
I know nothing of your grief, granted,
nor you mine, but isn't that why we're here?

No philosopher ever went into the deli
on Mercer & Spring and asked Mohammed
just to make her whatever sandwich

the universe had preordained. For once
we might exalt the significance of facts
and information. I hope to stop reliving

things I said once that were mildly funny,
and also stop being forced to organise
the populace in boxes, imagined boxes,

and heaping up these pyramids of objects
I do not need or love, and extracting
rotted bodies from the earth, a liquid

dead we latch and suckle hard upon
until the shrieking halts, until we grow
engorged as ticks, as cysts, and burst.

The Vocation

It's fair enough for a poet to have some dirt
beneath his fingernails
or a piece of leaf caught in her hair.

When you ask him how he's doing
it's fine for him to shuffle up
the bench a bit to let the ghosts sit down

or for her to pull a tangled length
of metaphor out of her pocket
to tie together all the losses.

It's more than normal for a poet
to choose the window while
the novelists prefer the aisle.

When poets turn on each other
they are like milk turning.
When they love

they are children with money.
They think their desk is an altar
and wearing a black sweater

speaks of perpetual mourning,
that staring at the ceiling is
an hour spent thinking

how the mundane deserves
its beautiful due, and in the wallet
of the poet sit the business cards

they've printed up declaring,
on one side, *the statement
on the other side is true,*

and on the other side,
*the statement
on the other side's a lie.*

The Politics of Feeling

I'm going to level with you now about the despicable phoniness of those
who declare they're going to level with you now: also, let me make it
abundantly clear that those who say let me make it abundantly clear

are shitting in your milk. There's a sickness at the core of this but
let them scream whatever they want: we will size it up beautifully,
we will size it up without frenzy or sloth or pretence. And let it be

noted that it has been noted. I am sitting here very still in the question
of myself, and by the time this poem appears I expect I will be even
whiter. As you are no doubt aware the Irish only recently got to be white,

but some of us seem to be liking it an awful lot. My sandwich is finished
but I sit on in the middle of the square, decentred by the lassitude of
Thursday and this recurring sinus infection. Abroad remains the trio

of affinities – the body one inhabits; God, the cause, or lack thereof, of all
level of outrageous detail; and the other animals who walk around me
endlessly in circles. The day has a superabundance of clarity: clouds erupting

out of their skin, whiteness on whiteness over the dogs in the dog run
growling and sniffing and crapping, over the jet of the fountain endlessly
replenishing the crest of itself in whitely continuous effort. The curled-up

leaves at your feet, desiccated reds and browns, patches of exhausted grass,
the Japanese jazz band, the texture and temperature of the bench. Why is there
this? For sensation? For pleasure? See if that stands up. I hold in my palm

a few at a time the facts of cashew nuts from the bag of facts of cashew nuts.
Everything already is fraying at the edges if not completely gone. Everyone
is mourned in turn and that stench is the stench of decay from the trash can.

Something rotting in a bag of skin. Look at it and away. If someone despises
you, the work is still to do nothing despicable, to be oppositional but
patient and cheerful as your own mother – if she wasn't pretending –

but what then? What is next? I no longer find it surprising that one of the wifi
networks coming up as my home option is ClassWar5G. Yesterday I noticed
another had appeared named PatrioticSocialist. I am telling myself to get up

and go when a guy slopes past pushing his kid in a stroller like I used to,
the lovely dullness of those intervals just shoving the stroller into the future.
On the next bench the squirrel surveils us, sits on its hunkers, munches.

I flick half a cashew off my sleeve and into infinity, and snap the Tupperware
shut, and stand up to brush myself off before walking out into Manhattan
like a good European as the rich get richer and the poor get fucked.

Inside Voice

What do I have to report?
He hands off his rucksack
     as we exit the elevator
and plucks the key from my hand
to take off at a clip down the corridor
swerving now
     and then out of sheer joy.
Even the way he eats I kind of find
     fascinating, chewing with a camel's
abstraction and giving his sister
the side-eye. I watch him as a lover
or as a mother might. He's as excited
     about my pasta and pesto
and grated cheddar cheese I've just
cut the mould off as he is about
Christmas, and if he seems to have sprung
from himself sometimes, other times
I watch him sit beside me in the pew,
bending his fingers back against the wood
as I used to do, and all attention to ceremony,
incantation, response, incense rising
in great drifts, dissolving, his
seriousness returned – and I think
here I go through but why if not
to testify against eternity and he
kneels beside me now as I kneel
here now beside him and talk to you

Pac Man

Katherine is three years old, and too hot, and utterly
decided not to let me tie the helium balloon
she got at Aminatou's party to her wrist.

She insists that she will hold it, and grips the ribbon
in her fist as I concede defeat and push the stroller
home through Soho's muggy afternoon.

The Used Bookstore on Wooster where the fat guy
in a woolly hat and a permanent rage works
is closing, and behind me, softly, *I want it back.*

Strange word for books that: Used. Manipulated.
Consumed. When I say we're alone with our thoughts
I mean all the gathered history and particulars

available to a single place in the universe,
called a light cone. Each occupies his or her
cell in the prison, and each is slightly unlike.

She was three for me for such a brief interval,
then four, five, ten, for almost nothing, almost
never. A pigeon flies from the scaffolding unnerved

by a shadow sliding of a sudden over the crosswalk,
wrinkling on pedestrians, a lugubrious bulldog,
and the shadow is cast by her balloon, Pac Man,

ascending rapidly to heaven. *I want it back*
and she adds, to clarify, *Now*, and offers me
a puzzled look to check I've understood.

Odd to watch the realisation take, up close,
like this, the central lesson of one-way loss –
and watch the knowing surface in her eyes as

hurt, unquestionably personal, and she is sobbing
now so loudly the bookseller, pricing up a stack
of vinyl, is watching from the counter.

I would get it back for you Katherine if I could.
All of it. The afternoon. The sun. The bulldog.
The traffic lights. The Libyan dry cleaner

with the gammy leg and speechless brother.
The cherry trees on Bleecker in their ordered
rows of frothy blossom and the yellow fleck

of Pac Man zipping upwards, almost gone.
I'd send it west, back across the sky to swallow
the luminous dot of the sun, and turn strobe-lit

and frenetic, for a moment or two deathless,
and have it hunt the bastard ghosts down
one by one by one until the grid is empty.

Mixed Marriage

Poetry's the art of introducing words
that haven't met & getting them to sit together
in a small room where they might fall –
improbably – in love – or try to kill each other –
or first one thing & later on the other.

Intermittently we felt it, the thready lining
under the small change & balls of fluff at
the bottom of the pocket of astonishment –
& the best of the rest of the time we kept
our heads down & tried to make sense

standing together & completely alone
while the words got along like a house
on fire, a street of houses, like the perfect
match had been struck and the cityscape's
erupting with sirens, collapsing in flames.

The Hudson River

Sekeena is really very sick and there is no way round it. In the boiler room where Eddie's hung the heavy bag we hit it, and he hits it pretty hard, and in between the grunts discuss the various Terror Management Systems open to him now. His essentially boils down to smashing things and building them back again into separate boxes and locking those boxes, and swallowing the key. Sekeena now is very sick.

Sekeena is not old enough to be very sick and her daughter is not old enough to have a mother who is very sick, and Sekeena represents the public of this island the Lenape knew as Mannahatta, where she defends the wretched, the huddled masses, the innocent, of course, and also grifters, assholes, shoplifters, muggers, murderers, rapists, that guy who pushed another guy in front of the subway at Columbus Circle – but Sekeena cannot be defended now from this.

I met Eddie at a party where he told a story up on stage, about when he was almost killed on Thompson Street by Latin Kings in an initiation, the initiation being you had to murder a random stranger. Eddie'd locked his bar up and was walking back toward his motorbike when one ran in at him from behind, and stuck a knife in him, and two ran in from either side and did the same, and left him for dead, but not before he knocked out the fourth, coming from the front, with a wild right hook. The surgeon put his chances of survival around three per cent, but look, he did, he made it, and here he is living. He doesn't understand why it couldn't have been him. He doesn't understand why it isn't him who's dying.

After hitting the bag in the basement Eddie and I get high on the roof of the five-floor walkup, having propped the fire-door with a brick, sitting in our plastic chairs on the asphalt amid the aerials and water towers. Tonight the city looks unpacked, laid out like components for some astonishing machine that the instructions have been lost for, and the sky is shot with pink and full of helicopters delivering billionaires to prostitutes or vice versa, and Eddie wants to know where one puts the rage, the outrage, how to box it up or pause it. How to kill it. The new Bishop of Wyoming came to see him to apologise for what the old Bishop did to him when he was nine years old. The worst that you can do.

think we choose our friends because the brand of madness is familiar to us, either from the mirror, or the genre of it is a type practised in that family also, and Sekeena is Canadian, hence pretty reasonable in some ways though not, it's fair to say, in all. Her father manufactured toys in Montreal though the family's Lebanese Muslim, and migrated west, like we all did, except Eddie, who came east. In the morning Sekeena's spending some time lying on the floor of the shower crying as her celebrated hair comes out in clumps.

I meet Eddie at Fanelli's where we sit at the bar, its glossy dark wood as worn as a banister and on its frontispiece – I had never noticed – the huge carved face of the Green Man, the forest dweller, the force that through the green fuse drives the flower, that drives the truck into the wall, the bike into the river, the cancer from the pancreas up into the liver, a motion and a spirit that impels all objects, all thought, and rolls through all things and so on, that drives the fist into the heavy bag or the face of a boy with a knife . . . How do you defend this? What quality of grace or mercy could adequately exculpate whoever perpetrated this? Sekeena, our defender, our writer and our reader, our mother and our sister and our daughter and our lover and our wife is very sick.

The hair of the Green Man looking out at our knees is made of delicately carved leaves, and he has apples for his cheeks, and when Eddie says touch wood, and we do, we are communing with the trees that stood here once and will again. Ghost forests of the past and future, all of the branches outstretched and empty. What I want from my friends is what I want from a poem, to share a space and time and feel you have been proximate to another's consciousness.

The week the state went into lockdown Eddie and I were meant to fly to Wyoming to pick up a pickup truck and drive her back from Laramie to New York. A mint green 1972 Ford F250 – a machine of harsh beauty, eight cylinders, three quarter ton payload. Longbed. Bench seat. Not mint green, Eddie says, but anti-establishmint green. We'd keep it upstate in one of the barns at Jay's place, in the mountains with the bears and the creek and the Trump signs in the yards, where we ended up waiting out that first lockdown.

Now Sekeena sits opposite, outside Blue Ribbon at a table on the pavement well away from everyone inside. Her eyes say, I am the one, I am the one: there is no way not to be me.

We are finishing twelve Chesapeake oysters when Eddie pulls up in the truck, Big Green, having driven from a film festival in Vancouver. He's in a documentary called Procession about therapy and the Catholic Church and child abuse. It's the first time I've seen the truck, and I go along for the ride through Soho and the Village to park it up over on the West Side. The cab feels like an engine room, and the truck shudders when Eddie turns the blade of the key, and the thing thunders awake and seems to enlarge, then chugs like a boat through Soho – and must be tacked and calmed and handled, managed – and we find at the garage on Chelsea Piers a space on the top storey, open to the sky. Eddie's telling me about the hospital receptionist, a righteous prick, who was explaining they had the wrong insurance and couldn't get the next set of scans without paying a deposit – immediately – of eleven thousand dollars. It's a warm night and we park at the edge and over there is the Hudson River, fast and unimpeded, churning darkness, and in the distance the water glitters with the lights of Jersey City.

Growing up there was a river two fields over. A tributary to the Ballinderry. Not large, it was persistent, a thing that mattered, since it lasted, and lasted since it changed. You couldn't quite look at it. The surface dragged your gaze along so you had to focus and refocus to hold the same spot. An object in motion is better in kind than an object at rest. The first refuses definition. The static dwindles, halts and rots, but that which is moving, that which continues to move, involves, perforce, eternity.

For the surgery, a distal pancreatectomy for adenocarcinoma, Dr Enrique Chabot needs multiple shots from the scans, and must get Diagnostic Imaging to burn them to CDs, and they found that having Eddie deliver them by hand between the hospitals was the fastest way to get the necessary information to him. Especially now with Covid, everyone is fucked and overloaded and short-tempered and Eddie has just emailed to tell me he felt like a Pony Express rider on the prairie there for a minute as he pulled up in Big Green, outside Sloane Kettering, clutching the bulging envelope.

Talking to the Sun in Washington Square

Looking after children means simultaneously building a field hospital,
a hedge school, a diner and an open-air prison with your bare hands
and operating them at a continual loss. In this instant they are playing

and you're sitting on a bench where the sun applies itself to the square
and you can feel it on your skin asking how it's been since you last touched,
and you tell her things are alright mostly, the sky is the epitome of sky,

the clouds give birth to themselves, the little people are getting even better
at belittling the bigger people, and you are done in now. You did your bit.
Birdwatching today in Central Park until you saw an osprey with a fish

in its beak and a splinter in a finger meant you had to all walk out and hail
a cab, and you saw the booth on sixth had its phone yanked off and wires
dangled. It took you to the endless conversation at dinner last night

about silence where your wife mentioned John Cage and the persistence
of absence in presence, or something, and the Mexican writer recited the noun
for quiet in four languages and you said nothing, offering, you thought,

the most evincive contribution. Now the sun is trying to tell you something
by splitting through the cloud like that. Some secret as to how its light
walks and flies at the same time, or why the nature of formations – clouds,

crowds, poems, marriage – is that they dissolve, and why there is such
an effort in just not. Heaven is a past participle of heave, the sun notes,
and the fountain stands to attention until she sets and it slumps to the pool.

You'd like to hear more about that sometime but not quite yet. You want
to know if all lives viewed from the inside present as a series of failures.
You want the side door held ajar a moment longer. This is the permacrisis,

sun. It is grim, the era of collapsing systems, of gaming the algorithm,
of the discontent late capitalism must inflict on us for it to thrive.
What you want is old friends who admit to complications not followers

or allies. The instantaneous personal magnetism of other people
is almost overwhelming sometimes – attractive or repelling.
The sun rests its hand on you and everyone and says, very softly,

Look how my light alights on the rock dove and the litter bin alike,
useless to corporations, meeting the froth of the cottonwood,
the bespectacled pianist, interstitial fauna, the angry kings of meth,

lovers solving the crossword, a Chinese student quietly crying,
all varying configurations of the code, and wait until I disappear
before you wander back in the way that fire wanders to make

an early dinner and clean up, to bath the children and tell them stories.

Anne Frank

The hair salon is called Who Cares and on Vigilstraat
the barrier says WELCOME IN THE SECRET VILLAGE.
I take a table on the pavement as the edible kicks in.
What is this implement called that's a fork and a spoon?
Yes. What if I saw myself in the spork and thought the face
remoter? Who was this anyhow? What's it for, why the dark?
What if we get there and the inn's already full? What if no
water gushes from the tap? We require details of the fire
all the same.
    The windows of the house across from yours
reflect the sun so viciously I cannot quite look at it although
later, in the square, a chain of giant bubbles made by a man
dressed as a medieval jester are billowing and wobbling
and the little children run through them screaming.

Curation

Consciousness is just the white noise
emitting from the vent, and has no bearing
on the workings of the air conditioning unit
distant in the basement.
                                Consciousness is just
the patrons clicking their heels on the parquet,
stopping at the painting the gallerist selected –

this, this all but monochromatic still life;
its objects set on a linen cloth in a kind of
tonal banquet – lead, then pewter silver
chalk slate bone –

the desolation overwhelming

                    until consciousness is just
distracted by this something else, the accent
of a few yellow tulips on the sideboard behind

         and consciousness moves outside to sit
on the hard bench as sunlight advances on
the rectangular lawn where the blades of grass
are slicing through to the visible.

For Vona Groarke

Sesame Street

There's no way to dress as a puppeteer.
Anything you wear is weird.

We tried watching the Elmo documentary
after Tom had left but I was too high.
My mind was shuffling itself, cutting in on itself.

Tom had just seen the documentary about the King of Pop
                              and those white
men who were learning to feel
something for themselves as
little children and Tom began recalling
being taken
into the bathroom
when he was three to

three two one

'perform fellatio'
on the twelve-year-old
his parents took in for a spell.

It's being processed.
Everything everything more
medication. Unhappily miscellaneous.
It was a kind of full distortion.
Finally, sentimental items.
Tom won't go back to Arizona.

He's off to meet a blue-eyed woman –
it's all taxonomies at this point –
and is sharing a car to Brooklyn
with my weed guy Asian Phil.

Asian Phil was Asian Phil
because White Phil worked the week.

Asian Phil did weekends and services
finance guys mostly,
doesn't get much 'old New York'.
Tom has left his wallet.

Why I thought of poetry
only this morning
walking through Penn station at
its most packed with the travelling intent
presences of these people I don't
know parting like flames before me

Ars Poetica, with the Salmon of Knowledge

Only I am standing here,
at the bathroom mirror
hacking at my lockdown hair

with the scissors
on my penknife
when I catch my eye –

and something like a poem
glances back
from the deep inside

but making out the grey figure
standing there
wielding a blade,

swims off immediately
and with good reason.
I would eat it for its secrets.

Fun for One

Taste wood. Taste stone. Taste
glass. Do you have a preference?

Leave the shape of your face
in every pillow in your apartment.

Listen to the sirens outside rising and falling.

When a thought comes that will lead you
into the past or future, dismiss it.

Sit at first light on a bench in the square
and stay completely still
until you begin to distinguish the calls
of all the different birds.
List those birds now in alphabetical –

Lie down for a while on the grass
with your arms wide
so you make the shape of a cross.
Face down the blank sky
and what you feel at your back
is the planet, the whole planet,
bracing itself.

At 4.25 p.m. make sure you face south-west.
No reason.

In your kitchen the function of the objects
is to re-establish your aloneness.

Watch the ant crossing the tundra
of your kitchen counter
confront the pool of water you spilt earlier.

Choose a new name for yourself.
I like Sonia Vogel. Or Nana Buttski.
Jonathanathanathan.

Draw the sound of the siren rising outside
with a coloured pencil or a biro.
Now draw the noise of a door opening,
now banging shut.

Ink a face on the palm of each hand
and flash them at yourself. Make one happy,
the other full of unspecified regret.

If you find the ant ascending the bread-bin
set your hand on said bread-bin
so that the ant steps onto your hand.
Look.

You are become the earth.

Try to look the ant in the eye.

Do ants have eyes?

Think about the ant thinking about you
thinking about it.

Hold your breath: first in air, then in the bath.

Longer, longer, longer.

Try to sleep sitting up. Try to sleep standing.
Try to sleep with one eye open.

Do ants sleep? Try to sleep with ear-plugs
and with Super Deep Brown Noise
and with the sirens outside

rising and falling
and rising.

Insert the biro like a rose
into the buttonhole
of your flannel pyjamas. Whisper into it
as if it is
a hidden microphone. You need
back up,
to be retrieved,
you need the team to come storming in.

Take a stack of these magazines and tear out
photographs of all the animals and arrange them
on the table
in scenes of loving harmony.

Make them eat each other.

Stand beside your desk and touch
wood
in order to commune
with the forest that stood once
where you stand now,
curls of birdsong, coins of sunlight
scattered on the leaf litter.

If the drain glugs in the sink imitate it.

If a dog barks on the street bark back.
If the siren rises and falls,
turn on the bathroom light
and look at your face in the mirror,
and keep on looking at your face
until your face is no longer your face

but the face of a stranger.

ii

Up Late

If I shut my eyes to the new dark
I find that I start to experience time
in its purest state: a series of durations
rising and dilating beneath my inwards gaze:
an eruptive core where the umbra blooms
in crestless waves of darkness as within
another umbra bubbles up from the interior –
from nothingness, from nowhere –
and at the centre of the crest of this
disintegrating, reassembling nest
the jet of time generates, is consciousness,
the planetary mind, aloft, alone, mine,
jostled and spun like a ping pong ball.

*

My father died today. Sorry to bolt that on.
You understand the shift required. This morning
the consultant said your father now is clawing
at the mask and is exhausted and we've thrown
everything we have at this. It's a terrible disease.

He promises to give him morphine and that a nurse
will be beside him at all times to hold his hand
and talk him through it.
                It being the transition,
the change of state, the fall of light, the trade,

the instant of the hand itself turning from the subject
into object. No, we are not allowed in the ward
and there cannot be exceptions. Thank you for making
this difficult call. But I know what the body wants.
Continuance. Continuance. Continuance
at any cost.

*

But dying, then, as we speak,
my father in the IC ward
of Antrim Area Hospital.

The icy ward.
The ICU.
I see you too.

On Sunday they permitted us to Zoom
and he was prone in a hospital gown
strapped to a white slab.

The hospital gown split at the back
and the pale cold skin of his back was exposed.

He lifted his head to the camera
and his face was dark red and puffy,
bisected vertically by the mask,

and we had to ask Elizabeth the nurse
to say his words back to us –
he sounded underwater –
it's been a busy day but not a good day.

*

I could see even with the mask on
your little satisfaction with the phrase
managed out.

And the achievement left you
so depleted you lowered your head
back to the slab, having done with us,

like some seal on a rock looking up
as we pass on the Blue Pool ferry
out to Garinish.
                        Dad,
you poor bastard, I see you.
You lay like that for a week alone
with your thoughts in the room.

Tethered. Breathless. Undefended.
At sea as on an ice floe
slipping down into the shipping lanes.

*

The eye adjusts, even to darkness,
even to the presence of what overwhelms us,
and as I make my way from the bed to the study
the soles of my feet on the carpet warp it
as any fabric made of this space-time will distort
beneath the force of a large object – and my father,
as it happens, is gigantic – and if you thought
an understanding could be reached, you are wrong
for it could not.
                          The goldfish pilots the light of itself
through a ten-gallon darkness and I keep watch
as the large hand of the clock covers the small
and leaves it behind to the weak approximation
I sit here in and finish writing.

                                        *

I want the poem to destroy time.
What are the ceremonies of forgetting?

There is a spring in Boetia
that lets the river Lethe enter our world.

King Gjuki's ale of forgetfulness.
Excessive phlegm.

But I like the notion of the angel
lightly tapping the baby

in its soft hollow above the top lip, erasing
all the child knows,

all its grief, all its terrible regret,
before it descends again fresh to the world.

*

After your stroke you were born once more
as smaller, greyer, softer, and after Mum died,
left bewildered, adrift, ordering crap online
and following the auctions, the horses, the football,
the golf – but hungering for company, for anyone,
sending money to that Kenyan who was younger
than me and flying out to Germany to see her,
and again, before Jackie arrived on the scene,
the bottle blonde who had 'her demons',
by which you meant she was a violent alcoholic,
although with Louise things seemed steady enough
for a few months, until you got stuck in one of
your loops about her ex-husband funding her
and the changing plans of an ingrate daughter –

*

You could never let anything go, a trait
I also suffer from, and kind of admire, but

that isn't possible here. The tick of the clock
is meltwater dripping into the fissure.

The minute hand clicks across the hour hand
and hovers for a minute, exactly,

and impinging on the vision is your slack wild face
and the way a nurse's hand might hold

your cold hand or try again to lift your hand
but your hand now will not respond.

*

I have been writing elegies for you all my life, father,
in one form or another, but now I find the path is just
this game trail through the forest, the forested mind,
which I must follow in the manner of an animal –
a deer, a fox, a chimpanzee – returning to the clearing
to nuzzle the corpse, to lick its nape or bite it softly,
to look away, and look again, and wait for a response.
One hand on the clock holds the other for a minute
before going on alone. It is death that is implicit
in the ticking.

*

One must negotiate the next moment. The mind
will not stop and certain things are good to think
with. Goldfish; carpet; clock. I want something fit
to mediate the procreative business of redoubling
the brittle world, and settle on an image, for a second,
since it is a given that the mind will keep returning
to the magic, the legerdemain, the trick: one hand
holding your hand as it turns into an object; as I turn
back along the track towards the fold, towards
the corner of the field where the father's body lies,
and with an animal's dumb clarity do grief work:
kiss your hand and kiss your cheek and leave
my forehead for a time pressed against yours.

*

When I phoned the hospital this afternoon
to say goodbye, though you were no longer lucid,

Elizabeth the nurse held the phone against your ear
and I could hear your breathing, or perhaps the rasping

of the oxygen machine, and I said what you'd expect.
I love you, Dad, and I want you to keep on fighting,

but if you are too tired now, and in too much pain,
then you should stop fighting, and let go, and whatever

happens it's okay. I love you. You were a good father.
The kids love you. Thank you for everything.

Then I hung up. And scene. Impossible to grieve
and not know the vanity of grief. To watch one

self perform the rituals that take us. Automaton
of grief, I howled, of course, by myself

in my office, then sobbed for a bit on the sofa.
An elegy I think is words to bind a grief in,

a companionship of grief, a spell to keep it
safe and sound, to keep it from escaping.

There are various ways to memorise.
Plato calls on Mnemosyne.

My grandfather Bertie liked to tie
a knot in his blue handkerchief.

My father wrote in biro on his palm.
I cannot leave the poem alone.

*

Do you remember the pure world? I remember it
from being a kid. All was at stake in that place,
one moved through it sideways, through forests
of time, lost in them, and had to be called back
to the moment. Infinities growing in stone,
in moss, in the hayshed, the rain, the wind,
in the darkness under the cattle grid.

Rilke says of the pure unseparated element –
                '. . . someone dies and *is* it.'

*

It's after two.
You're dead by now I hope.
Who thought to write that?

But there's no hurry now,
no effort, no need to call.
You might be only sitting

in your red chair
endlessly flicking
through the channels.

*

When I asked the doctor, Andrew Black, he said,
it could take minutes, it could take hours,

and I see you slumped, your eyes shut,
propped against some pillows.

Something in you finally given up
defying gravity, some obedience

to objecthood settled in you now
and set up home. Set in stone.

Outside on the motorway the headlights
of the vehicles are necklaces of diamonds,

double-strung, and trailing westwards
alongside them, the necklaces of garnets.
                                                    Dad,
I cannot stay in the room with you too
long in my mind. It is too hard. I thought

there would be futurity. I thought things
would happen. Nothing major. Barbecues.

Why barbecues? God knows. You are walking
round Bantry at the Friday market in your shorts

in the light rain, your white tube socks pulled up
and a bright T-shirt from some Spanish golf course

tucked into your shorts. By the way, Dad,
we are even – you and I. No need. Look:

How absolutely still the room is. Outside
the widowed sky has grown huge with stars.

The Milky Way meandering like the Ballinderry
though the night has come with work to do.

It sits with you and broods. It wants you to come
at your own pace. And in the next moment

you might get up and speak clearly to everything,
creation, extinction, infinities rising within you.

*

Alastair Laird is dead. Fuckety fuck. Fuckety
fuck fuck fuck fuck. My dad is dead. Bad luck.
The light breaks and the night breaks and the line
breaks and the day is late assembling. Rows
of terraced houses are clicking into place. Clouds
decelerate and make like everything is normal:
the children wanting porridge, voices forcing
pattern out of circumstance, pitching rhythmic
incident on little grids of expectation, satisfaction,
disappointment, this new awe, and walking to
school, at the corner where the halfway house is,
leaves animated in a briefest circle by the wind.

i.m. CAEL
11.03.2021

iii

Night Sky in Tyrone

Maybe birds provide the eyes the dead look out of.
Or is it knots in furniture they queue up at

to spy from, bickering, whispering with shock
how grey her hair is now, how skinny he has got.

My sister thinks that portly robin on the lawn
is Dad come back to say hello, and he takes a little hop

out of sunlight into shade before alighting on
the compost bag and lengthily explaining everything

that we can see is his, his apple tree, his grass,
that patch of rhubarb he'd been about to cut back.

Why not. We finish up a bottle then another
and the evening's coming on, and then the night is here,

and we sit out underneath so much made known
that's always there – the depths of emptiness and fire.

Basically Adidas

She'd found his other phone
hidden under the bathroom sink,
and the empty bottles of own-brand vodka

stashed in the grass bin
of the broken lawnmower,
and said he'd already had two strikes

and that was three, and she was done,
and I was sat here listening
in the car in the dark in the rain,

the side of my head pressed against the glass,
parked up on Hopefield
waiting for Harvey to come out of Scouts,

but thinking of our father and me
driving round town with a boot full
of packets of navy tracksuits

he got cheap from some guy who worked
in Desmonds factory shop
in Swatragh.

I would set my head against the glass
just like this
as the Ford Granada sailed round the estate

and Dad is standing on the doorstep
talking to Richie Smith –
So what it is

is they're basically Adidas,
they're made the same,
but they have these two stripes instead of three.

Attention

is a single white marble, translucent with a turquoise wave
breaking within it, attention is that marble bouncing wildly down the alley
and reaching the top of the steps by the bar I met you at in Monti,
Martino, to sit out the evenings drinking on those steps, where all the treads
are bowed in the middle by millennia of pilgrims heading up
to San Pietro in Vincoli, to seek forgiveness, to bow their heads, to ask
some questions of themselves in a place attention is a single block
of white Carrara marble carved by Michelangelo into the statue of Moses
we stood before, stoned, wondering why he'd horns, and attention
to the style of things is an attribute worn, Martino, by you around Hoxton
or Testaccio like a purple boiler suit, which you also wore,
and attention is that single white marble now descending the stone steps
by the bar, rolling along the depth of one tread and dropping, then
rolling the depth of another, and dropping, and the next, dropping and
rolling, dropping and rolling, not silently, until the single white
marble, translucent with a turquoise wave, hits the pavement and skitters
onto the cobbles to wedge, pearl-like, beneath the tyre of a Vespa.
Martino, it is evening and raining in London, and I am making tea and we
don't say that we both know it is the last time we will meet. Your face
is swollen from the treatment and your head fantastically stitched together
as you sit on the edge of the sofa, all attention, all wrapped in chains
of attention. *I vincoli* can be translated as constraints, bonds, ties, links. Or
limits, obligations. The chains of St Peter, the rock of the church, sit
in a mother-of-pearl box Freud walked past to stand before the Moses statue
he writes is *seated; his body faces forward, his head with its mighty
beard looks to the left, his right foot rests on the ground, and his left leg is raised
so that only the toes touch the ground.* What the statue says to me
is that Moses can barely stop himself, that he almost cannot bear it,
is on the verge of rising and allowing something overwhelming – rage,
I think – free rein, and impatiently he stares down tourists traipsing past,
outfacing them as he outfaced Freud, who came every afternoon for weeks

to try to disentangle the piece's emotional effect. *Attention*, from the Latin
ad tendere, to stretch towards, to try to meet, and Tino, in your brain
the tumour spread so fast it has taken the shape in the scan of a finch, a finch
in flight, and has pecked away your mind to such an extent you can write
still but no longer read, and as you sit in the kitchen attending, attending, all bound
up in these chains of attention, all charged with a terrible, helpless
attention, I want to tell you Michelangelo is reputed to have loved the statue
so much he hurled his hammer at it and cried that it would not speak.

i.m. *Martino Sclavi*

Border County Pastoral

There is a grid of light coming through the iron grilles
onto whitewashed walls in the parish hall.

We'd like to thank the ladies for the lovely spread.
                    They always do us proud.
Our purpose here is to serve
sandwiches. Traybakes.

As a rule we tend to like sportswear more
than sports. Uniforms, yes. Or a boiler suit
with cowshit caked on the left knee
or a hairnet for the boning line,
a sweater for the vestry since it gets
very nippy in here in the evenings.

We attend the beetle drive.
The swimming gala. The harvest service.

We drive Norman to the pub for opening
so he can drink himself to death.

That cousin is in Glasgow or in Dublin
or in Houston married to a radiographer
or a videographer or a pyramid seller.

We love Ryan but he's a bad drunk.

And we know them by sight, aye,
but not by name

though we used to stick that one, goose-grass,
to the backs of the girls' jumpers in primary school,
and that one, giant hogweed, is poison.
We had a rash off it once pulling it out by the stream,
and the dock leaves of course for nettles.

Once up in Portrush we are dared by them,
by the girls, to go in for a night swim
and then they are gone, long gone
with our clothes, and our jokes, our ages,
our names,

and with the whole town spilling out from the pubs
we have to run back to the caravan
in only our keks.

Politics

Standing at pump four
of the garage in Ballydehob,
filling the Honda with diesel,
I want the counter to stop
at a round number, a whole euro,
so if the tank's getting full
and the flow's clicking off
I restart, easing out my finger
then tightening the trigger
until the digit ticks to zero.
I like to iron a white shirt
on mornings I'm hung over.
Sometimes I button it right
to the neck, neat-like. Unsure
exactly what it is I'm meant
to ask forgiveness for,
I do so anyway, but also want
this loud unpleasant static
on the speakers as my coffin
penetrates the curtain,
like when my mother's did.
Sometimes I can barely
keep my mother shut. I mean
my mouth. I know that every
evil act I ever saw committed
had at its core identity.
Like when they exploded David
and our windows shook, it was
because of who he was, of what
skin he was born in. On call,
Ernie was among the first

to reach the scene, and told me
there was one torso lodged in
the fork of a tree, and it had not
been possible to identify them all
and that's one kind of irony, yes.

Alone: the TV Show

(from the Danish)

Off they sail and then I stand on the shore
companionless. In shock. Now must I adopt
the custody of self. When all of the adrenaline
has slowed so should I build my shelter.
If it rains much I get wet and then cold
and then dead – but shut up look about!

My domain is everywhere and my purpose
to survive it. The private and professional
undertakings I renounced just because
I want this, 200%. I have all of the surplus
and the sharp equipment. I am very real.
Never have I been before to the extent.

Finding pleasure in just – not to have to be
something other one than what one is.
The energy goes up and I grow totally happy
in the lid. It really just occurred as reasonable
cunningly. If the world might know now
it should not start to mess here with me.

I eat bark of pine for four days. Five.
And endeavour not to have. Wind opposes.
The tournament I signed for to reconcile
with every living part and in particular
my father who is dead. A question is this
tension life occasions in the mind.

Idiot of culture distracting and misleads.
Just as every fit does not, a counterfeit
of face. Count these very ribs. In some sense

I live inside. And if the thinks are licensed
they dominate and fear. A large bear left
these by the shelter. It does not negotiate.

O nature. Such is the fuck. Crisis management
of earthworm rations and hard angles.
My cutting sense is a fear experience –
at the snares twisting round to trees
looming yes. Those behind the trunks
move as I move then breathe when I do.

It thusly gives me blood on the teeth
to dwell so like on this. There is no reason
to expose myself to more. It does not please
to live me. Although things there are deeper
those to find in life, and this a good place
for that, it has affected me very mood-wise.

What music I make with this pebble and stick.
Hours of that. Ice at night in the bay cracks,
sore vexed. It is brain dead sour right here.
Wow. It is the hard now. All downhill faster
sharply gone and squashed in half to thinning
point. Interiors grow weighted as the mountain.

Totality of night winds up here lisping.
Extremest forest dark. Snappage underfoot.
Branches catch in hair and at the clearance
moon delivered light and more on the breath
overhead adrift where farthest stars listen.
I am absolutely here but not what that mean.

The Outing

The magpie reasserts its stance
with a testy flap of black on white,
a flash of blue, and a stone might do

but doesn't so I have to shoo it off
with a folded tartan picnic blanket
and the baby rabbit –

what is left of it – keeps screaming –
and it happens that your options narrow
sometimes drastically

and what you might do if the kids
were not here is walk to the car,
and get in it and leave, turning up

the radio, but they want to know,
now, what one does with enormous
pain when you see it, where

you should put it, how might you
stop it, and they're watching,
and the rabbit is done, past saving,

so I lift the stone again and the bird
hops off as I walk across, and looks on
with interest, and if at first I miss it

the second time smashes in the socket
of the rabbit's eye, the one the magpie's
already emptied out to a plush red nest,

a divot of flesh. I'm in the driver's seat
and breathing and need to drink some water.
I can overhear its screaming in the silence

that fills the car on the drive back to a house
that is a little different; harder, sharper,
and where my children will not look at me.

Modest Proposal

By means of this enchanted stone
I promise to transform you to a hostile asshole
or failing that a fake-nice nauseating cretin.

Stare into its inky depths and find yourself
reflected back mesmerised by your reflection.

What I propose is to coach you into thinking
other people are not really people
and you have no duty to them,

and I mean to train you into piling onto
any victims or unfortunate misfits that come your way,
because you fear the real pain social shunning brings,

or watch with satisfaction from the sidelines chanting
Fight, fight, fight.

The other person's face is what prohibits us from killing
but I will furnish your world solely
with the images of faces – avatars, puppets –

and offer not real rewards
but merely symbols of rewards
and this will make no difference.

Here is a raised thumb. A yellow circle
bearing two black dots and a sickle-like slash.

What I posit is to gift you the very barest life:

strangers will bring you food;
algorithms choose who you should date
or imitate, idolise, despise;

and the addiction can be hidden for a bit
but your disposition shifts, your real sorrow
only deepens –

and you will try to justify it
as the price of this, this sorcery
promising an end to having to hear yourself
think. Rise on the wave of fresh
outrage and tap into a kind of rhythm
established on distraction, compulsive
pecking at the soul's scabs, a hankering
for affirmation, and growing ever more
engrossed with portentous events
invisible to those sitting in the room with you.

Even the gods need a break from themselves
and choose to assume the shape of a swan,
a shower of rain or a burning bush –
but you'll remain yourself, stridently
identified, tending that projection,

repeatedly seeking your suffering,
forking the witching charm from your pocket
to scrutinise it hard and walk into
a lamp post

for what I propose is to re-purpose
the entirety of your existence,
and leave you sitting there staring,
furious, inert.

The Inheritance

Bellman's auctioneers in Horsham have listed in their coming auction
a terracotta rhubarb forcer, which I'm pretty sure I'd find a use for,
if only in this poem, though what I most require is a universal squirrel

baffle, what with all the hassle these two squirrels that like scrapping
in my mulberry are giving me with feeders, the peanut feeders,
the cheeky fuckers. One is sat defiantly here on the fence, adjusting

and readjusting a chestnut in its paws, a chestnut still embedded
in its spiky helmet, which it solves, splitting the pith with its teeth
to unconceal the conker's extraordinary brown. He nibbles on that

for a bit and then stops, and meets my eye with his typical stare,
the staring contest he likes to dare me to, and lose. The mulberry
leaves have some kind of rust spot disease I should ask Fari about,

Fari who's my next-door neighbour from Persia, who likes to garden
in a caftan and smoke anorectic cigarettes between her pots of
fresh mint tea. The squirrel scampers along the fence, descends

the trellis to bury the chestnut in the flowerbed and I remember
how I told my father, in one of our last phone calls,
that I had spent the day in the garden, pulling up ground elder,

and had come across a few chestnut saplings sprouting where
the squirrels must have buried conkers and forgot them,
and he had wanted to know what I did with the plants,

the chestnut saplings, and told me I should have sold them,
that those things were worth money . . . In the end it took five days
and six skips to empty out my father's house, his many mansions:

hummel plates, decanters, boxes of jars, of pens, eleven artificial
Christmas trees, several thousand miniature bottles of liquor
he kept on the shelves in the garage, and I was overwhelmed

then and am again by all the stuff, the bits and bobs, the clobber –
a terracotta rhubarb forcer, a universal squirrel baffle –
and there was this plastic bottle of pink raspberry bubble bath

that sat on the bath since my mother bought it, maybe thirty years
back from Poundland or B&M Home Bargains since it matched
the pink towels, and I have been looking at it ever since I started

coming home from university to that house, and lying in the bath
looking at the same almost full bottle of pink raspberry bubble bath
that outlasted both of them, my parents, and is in some landfill

now near Pomeroy outlasting us. Sometimes I don't want to shape
the contours or unpick the hard entanglements, I don't want to be
involved or responsible at all. I would like to use my teeth to split

the pith and stare at that man watching from behind the glass. Sip
water from the birdbath and step so lightly on the parched grass
of this tiny patch in Kilburn, each blade might yet remain upright.

Vespers at Pacifico's

The others have no interest
in the slightest
but those are swifts
dipping down
to lift off milli-sips
of kinking noon-light
on the surface now
re-rippled by the beak
one forks at the closest
interstitial moment
to snip the pool minutely.
The tail is short
compared to the swallow
and a swift has scythe-like
wings – it cannot land
so spends its life aloft,
declining, sometimes,
into mine. A woodpecker
makes itself distinct
from a distance.
Its brisk retort
on dead oak trunk
is instinct, and this
its district, and this
its call to order,
its palate cleanser.
Nothing but a woodpecker
organises so much
personal force in such
a tiny space, then quits.
It flits again, is gone

quick and then alights
high in the cedars
behind the pavilion.
There is this energy.
Bewildering.
Abruptly cicadas
in concert switch
off, and it's only
endless till it's not,
till the sun consents
and bats come.

Privilege

I was working as a lawyer in Poland for a large firm trying to cash in on the deregulation of the Eastern European markets when I visited the brush shop.

It was on a side street in the shadow of our skyscraper, the first in Warsaw. I didn't spend much time in the office, especially in the afternoons. I liked to wander past an empty woman's boutique called Troll, an empty sports shoe store called Athlete's Foot.

I'd walked past the brush shop – no sign – several times before I entered, ringing the bell on the door. Wooden counter. Wooden floor. Three assistants in shopcoats talking, and continuing to talk. The shop sold only brushes, but brushes of all kinds: toothbrush, bottlebrush, hairbrush, broom. A bristle brush for fur. A shaving brush. A universe of brushes hung on nails on the back wall. The assistants persisted in ignoring me but in a way that was not, it felt, purposeful: their lack of interest was entirely genuine. I decided to buy a dustpan and brush, and I gestured. They could sell me the brush, but they couldn't sell me a dustpan, no. For the dustpan I would need a pan shop.

When I went home the fever started. I sweated through the sheets and grew delirious and sat up once, convinced there was a large black scorpion on my chest crawling up towards my neck. I screamed and leapt out of bed and kept trying to brush it off my chest.

I sat out on the balcony at night, smoking, wrapped in a duvet. Ulica Bonifraterska. I'd lived in that street for almost a year before Bartosz mentioned the wall had run down the middle of it, enclosing the ghetto I'd been walking out of every morning.

Ode on the Adult SoulUrn

I possess now approximately a fourth of each of my parents
standing in massive mostly empty pewter canisters
from Amazon on the edge of the lowest bookshelf by my bed.

It is only the usual universal deeply particular normal
sad ridiculous basic absurd. I didn't check the size
before I ordered them, the urns,[1] for next-day delivery

to the undertaker in Cookstown, Bryan Steenson,
a few years below me in school, whose own father
was the undertaker before him, Robin, and also a driving

instructor, my driving instructor, and my sister's before
that, and Bryan said, coming through from the back room,
they're rather large, and indeed they were.[2] Torpedoes

cradled in his arms. Military shells. Slightly fascistic-looking,
futuristic-looking huge steel urns[3] I set on the back seat
of the Focus and, having fastened their seat belts,

---

1. Pewter Large Adult Urn for Human Ashes – A Beautiful and Humble
Urn for Your Loved Ones Remains. This Lovely Simple Urn Will Bring You
Comfort Each Time You See It – with Velvet Bag.

2. BEAUTIFUL & DURABLE – Handmade and designed to represent
your everlasting love, this cremation urn with Beautiful Pewter Finish,
durable and built to last. Suitable for humans of all sizes up to 200lbs and
can also be used for the cherished remains of pets.

3. HAND CRAFTED WITH A STUNNING PEWTER FINISH – The
superior craftsmanship and materials that have gone into making this
cremation urn ensures the ashes of your loved one are completely protected
and given the upmost of respect.

drove back to the Malone Lodge on Eglantine Avenue,
having determined to decant them – my parents –
into Tupperware containers I'd stopped and bought in Asda

in Cookstown, since I would never fit a pair of urns[4] this
enormous in my carry-on, and as I kneeled in the empty bath,
as I kneeled down fully clothed in the bath and arranged

my mother's Tupperware, and started shaking out her urn,
the nitty gritty, the silt, the slick kibble, the salt and pepper,
it was awful – so I stopped that and decided to abandon

my running shoes instead to fit the urns in the case.
At security in Aldegrove I was pulled aside, though the fact
that they were tactful, the security men, I don't mention

before I like to describe how they swabbed both my parents
for drugs was it or explosives. I wish she had smoked some
weed, my mother, or taken mushrooms or a line of coke.[5]

You could see her old high school from the big window
of the hospice room in Newry, and when the pain became
really just unbearable, the lovely nurse had told her to think

---

4.   GIVE YOUR LOVED ONE THE QUALITY THEY DESERVE – When
you've lost someone close you need a premium quality urn to hold their
ashes and act as a fitting tribute to the love you shared. This beautiful crema-
tion urn is handcrafted to give your loved one's remains the superior quality
they deserve.

5.   THIS URN WILL LEAVE YOU COMPLETELY SATISFIED OR FULL
REFUND – SoulUrns is a Brand who cares for you, your family, and your
late loved one. If for any reason you are not completely satisfied, just return
it for a full refund.

about some other place entirely, a landscape meaning peace,
just an absolute happiness and feeling of calm,
and she said she'd picked as hers a field of lavender,

and you could see that she was helped by that, was happier,
and had she ever seen such a thing in real life,
some summer night driving up for the ferry through France,

warm air streaming from the passenger window wound
a few inches down, the dusk beginning, us children asleep
in the back and the green fields giving way to a sudden dark,

these lanes of lavender, waves of lavender shadow growing
darker in their blueness, into their blue darkness, layers
of darkness, I don't know, and won't now, and I lay there

in the empty bathtub thinking about that for a fair while

with the urns, heavy old things, hugging them to me.

The Call

I'm registered dead
but the man on the line
is called Maurice
and lives in Bangladesh.

I'm registered dead
but Maurice explains
that the company running
the site is a third party

and I've reached him
at the company that set it up,
which is very different,
and I must speak to someone else.

I'm registered dead
but Alison in Belfast tells me
I need the second and fifth
letters of a password

I don't remember having set
in order to enter
the kingdom, and also
a memorable date

I cannot guess although
I suggest the date of my
death, which is today,
they say, and just then

my dead mother
comes on the line
and tells me to quit
with all that yapping.

Feedback

Hidden by the froth of apple blossom the squirrel chirps at some affront,
and at the skylight a bee is trying to get out by going up, which won't do;
the sun is staring down hard from the bluest sky, and all the trees and plants

strain outwards, upwards, as they must, and sanity perhaps is just ability
to punctuate, and the poem a simple way of saying something complicated,
or the other way around, and anyhow is tantamount to happiness, to be only

where I am – and if I do not love the rock doves strutting mindlessly about,
cooing stupidly, forever looking at me with the side-eye, well, pigeons will be
pigeons always and coming to my lawn, and if I focus on their neckerchiefs

of purple tinged with emerald, there is something there to be connected, plus
something in the way the hose in ever-wider yellow loops negotiates the grass
is how I might extend myself, extend what's meant by 'us', that word the poet

Oppen thought each person must define, alone, and the grass is dead and brown,
and everything is happening much faster than expected, but my work is seasonal,
and this is the kind one does in spring, when everything is meant to be returning,

and the experts were all right, and then were not alright; concerned, worried,
stunned, aghast – despairing – and I read once flabbergasted, all the experts
flabbergasted at how the losses multiply, and wait to devastate, and the wheels

are coming off the thing even if this bee persists against the glass, and the squirrel
shakes the blossom as it moves through, still sore, but it is I that am nothing today,
it is I that put away my grief, and reader, as you go about your afternoon or evening

be sure to send my best – please give my love I mean – to every one, to every thing.